A High Plains Year in Haiku

Art Elser

Illustrations by
Eileen Roscina

WalkerDoodle Press

Also by Art Elser

We Leave the Safety of the Sea

A Death at Tollgate Creek

As The Crow Flies

To See a World in a Grain of Sand

It Seemed Innocent Enough

Memoir

What's It All About, Alfie?

A High Plains Year in Haiku

Haiku by Art Elser
Illustrations by Eileen Roscina

WalkerDoodle Press

Copyright © 2021 Art Elser
All rights reserved.

Illustrations by Eileen Roscina
Copyright © 2021 Eileen Roscina

No part of this book may be reproduced or transmitted in any form or by any means, electronic or mechanical, including photocopying, recording, or by any information storage and retrieval system without the expressed written permission of the author, except in the case of brief quotations in critical articles and reviews.

ISBN-978-0-9984554-8-8

WalkerDoodle Press
Denver, Colorado

As always for Kate

ways that I love you
I'll start by counting the stars
in the milky way

One sees clearly only with the heart.
Anything essential is invisible to the eyes.

> The Fox, *The Little Prince*
> Antoine de Saint Exupery

backyard surprise
season's first flutterby
a cabbage white

                    spring sunrise
                    with primrose clouds
                    first robin song

a cooler day
yesterday's crocuses
have closed up shop

six-thirty
light breaks softly east
bearing hope

                        crocuses sing
                        yellow and lavender songs
                        to welcome spring

April prairie
pronghorn does in small herds
pregnant with twins

        soft April sun
        paints verdant hills with shadows
        prairie morning

open mic readings
brilliant poetry workshop
two days in heaven

Mom's old peach tree
half dead
but . . . ah . . . blossoms

                        morning contrail
                        feathered by nature's brush
                        her blue canvas

fifty sparrows
flitting from tree to tree
gone in a blink

                    on the grassland
                    song of meadowlarks
                    melody of spring

          our neighbor's children
          search the lawns for treasures
          Easter egg hunt

spring surprise
the year's first dragonfly
lapis magic

the hawthorn blooms
first white and then turns pink
blushes into spring

tonight's huge moon
slips through a tangle of trees
climbs in beauty

        storms grumble past
        take their anger elsewhere
        weather warnings

in the fountain
a yellow and black splash
goldfinch drinks

gray skirts of rain
drape from ominous clouds
that spit lightning

                      last night's raindrops
                      diamonds on the peach tree
                      in the morning sun

as I shave
a gray-haired old man
watches

                our walk bejeweled
                with jonquils
                joy fills the day

I pick up gifts
left for me by my pup
Sir Poopsalot

at five-ten AM
full moon peeks in the window
to make sure I'm up

women's voices
fill the nave's silence
with joy and hope

a child took my hand
asking me to read to him
a joyous gift

                        two AM
                        the bedroom's awash
                        in snowlight

        my neighbor paints
        and smiling blue pansies
        spring from her brush

the linden
seasons the morning air
with sweetness

                         scumbled sky
                         thins from the sun's warmth —
                         high cirrus

the sky at dusk
drains from pale blue to gray
conjures a bat

where earth meets sky
the diaphanous moon
a pale wafer

low morning sunlight
sets the peach blossoms aglow
like alabaster

                      quiet morning
                      cool with fog and mist
                      crows circle low

crystals of dew
brilliant in the peach tree —
bring morning joy

                inline skater
                poetry in motion
                fluid graceful

bare street corner
sprouts vines with heart-shaped leaves
morning glories

winter's unlocked
snowmelt sings in downspouts
finches in trees

                    passing ambulance
                    my dog's howling visible
                    in the freezing air

there . . . in the south
Jupiter leads Saturn
Earth's bright brothers

        loud happy chatter
        a shadow becomes a bird
        cheery goldfinch

a tiny black ant
zig-zags the bathroom tiles
its endless search

Sunday choir
chickadee and finch voices
bless the day

                              the spring day
                              fills with purple scent
                              lilacs

light spills
into the bathroom sink
full moon

                    cumulus herd
                    stampedes off the mountains
                    wild in the wind

in the silence
across a wide green field
a bugle cries

                              as day fades
                              spring's first bats flutter —
                              wife's primal fear

overnight the hills
have slipped on their spring shirts
of lime green

                as I drive home
                a faint glow in the clouds
                hints of the moon

Degas'
sketches pastels paintings
what joy

liquid moonlight
pours in the window
fills half the sink

hovers and flits
sips nectar from hostas
hummingbird moth

Wyoming late spring
prairie grasses lush and green
colts fawns calves and wind

        today is the day
        we remember and honor
        those who gave their all

    the pup and I
    bask in the backyard sun
    scent of lilacs

this morning dawn
wears a sheer cirrus blouse
soft spring light

a pair of geese
waddle across busy street
drivers watch . . . wait

all day with poets
talking writing poetry
the day glows with joy

                    bright first quarter moon
                    sails high in the April sky —
                    scent of mock orange

at sunset's edge
of a periwinkle sky
a thin pink blush

a song frolics past
adding joy to the day
goldfinch tune

                                        April's full moon
                                        peeks in and out of clouds
                                        follows me home

Venus glows bright
in fading evening light —
a crescent moon

                          a little girl
                          in her princess outfit
                          her father's joy

joyous music
from a roadside ditch
chorus frogs

spring sunrise —
sky flushes pale orange
with faint robin song

                crocuses
                cheer our drab alley
                nature's gift

now the tulips
open their orange throats
to join spring's song

                front glides off
                clouds thin to gossamer
                air is feather soft

the poet wrote
"there will come soft rains"
they fell last night

need that special tool
it's not in either toolbox
buy new . . . find the old

alley butterfly
lands and lets me get close —
mourning cloak

morning is filled
with the silence of snow
then a finch sings

                    awakened at two
                    by the sound of passing geese
                    ancient vernal calls

short green leaves
spear through garden dirt
soon daffodils

on the walk
a cicada waits
for the sun

puffy clouds drift
off the mountains and melt
into a blue sea

wildfire smoke
veils the summer sky
hides the mountains

                wildfire smoke
                now comes from Canada —
                has no passport

      the red planet
      glows in the summer night
      its crystal cities

slow graceful flight
white cruciform shape
snowy egret

morning breezes
dance in the tree tops
aspen leaves clap

the mice have built
a tiny garden kingdom
we need a cat

        small brown butterfly
        on tattered native thistle
        guzzling nectar

doe and fawn graze
unaware I sit and watch
I stand they run

you there cricket
chirping at my window
why your loud silence

three small mice
not blind and had their tails
feast on spilled seeds

last night's cricket
hasn't sung tonight
has he found love

                        in evening dusk
                        turquoise and bright coral
                        Navajo sunset

three AM
one cricket singing
sounds lonesome

morning of the fourth
a swallowtail stops for death
beautiful still life

                perched on the back gate
                cooper's hawk
                trolling for song birds

a woodpecker drums
as mother young daughter watch
their faces aglow

                        amid chittering birds
                        the quiet flutter
                        of a swallowtail

dragonfly pair
bless the soft morning light —
angel-bright wings

wildfire smoke
drives me inside today
sneezing . . . honking

Sunday morning walk
awash
in joyful bird-song

last night's sunset
cast an orange glow —
wildfire smoke

                        two crows on branch
                        one scolding the other
                        old married pair

at thistle feeder
goldfinch with his black beret
sings as he flies off

so much joy
two days of writing
so many friends

in thin cirrus
a pale quarter moon speared
by a contrail

under feeder
squirrel and junco
cleanup crew

        the vision clinic —
        frightened Asian woman waits
        for a translator

    earthshine lights
    barely visible moon
    cradled in silver

high morning sky
gauzy in thin cirrus
old airman daydreams

morning fog
lifts into pastel blue sky
laced with cirrus

we meet to break bread
with an old friend and his wife
bread of great joy

                        on the patio
                        a large beautiful moth
                        an evening's gift

an ancient blue spruce
sighs
in the morning breeze

                              a crow caws
                              asks for the sun to rise
                              robins join in

there . . . stalking me
as I walk down the street
my moon shadow

                        the darkness
                        nicked by the moon's edge
                        bleeds lightly

at the clinic
the wind stirs tawny grass
its graceful dance

two silver trails
crisscross the garden walk
exploring snails

        clouds echo light
        from tonight's gibbous moon
        beautiful night

fireworks at dusk
revive ancient memories
Quang Ngai and Tet

                        flash of gold
                        tiger swallowtail
                        flutter of joy

one scoop waffle cone
on hot July afternoon
my inner child laughs

mother and toddler
romp and laugh and love with joy
others stare at phones

                        as I drive home
                        from my poetry group
                        peach tinted sunset

loud murder of crows
silences
into neighborhood trees

                    mountains west
                    are born with the sun
                    rise from earth

the morning's clean blue
is littered
with cirrus feathers

a single contrail
stitches the afternoon sky
white thread on blue silk

in night's silence
the sad voice of a flute
sings someone's pain

wind blows fall leaves
that spin and hiss on streets
rivers of gold

                    our daughter's home —
                    she brings a ton of joy
                    and bushels of smiles

fall stopped by today
and left a business card
bright red maple leaf

a dragonfly
hovers to say farewell
to summer

        a crow
        calls once to greet the sun
        then silence

a hungry crow
in Starbucks' parking lot
eats his breakfast

                windblown leaves
                scrape and hiss in street
                sounds of drought

    soft peach clouds
    light the autumn morning
    blessing the day

here and there a leaf turns
gold
in an ocean of green

                                      last night's raindrops
                                      slip back into the air
                                      as soft mist

locust trees
drop gold on the grass
fall treasure

        the sky alight
        pink to orange burnt red
        Blue Ridge sunset

a raucous screech
from the ponderosas
bluejay's call

high winds sculpt
sky's lenticular shapes —
storm's a-brewing

dawn tiptoes in
wearing a pale blue gown
light pink slippers

granite boulder
softened by dappled sun
and children

                  two bluejays stop
                  to drink from our fountain —
                  they're headed south

we wade through
spring and summer sunlight
on fall walks

a bullet flies
from shadow to sunburst
flash of goldfinch

                this autumn day
                with lenticular clouds —
                its lace mantilla

three weeks of fall
and light frost on the roof
winter's first kiss

                        under feeders
                        feeding on spilled seeds
                        dark-eyed junco

there dead in the grass
black feathers white spots red eye —
a spotted towhee

three porcupines
sit in a cottonwood
quilting haiku

bright bits of sun
from top strands of a fence
mountain bluebirds

mismatched socks
oh! here's another pair
mismatched too

this day I help
honor a friend who's flown west
vaya con dios

a waterfall
splashes into the creek
above the koi pond

this fall's leaf fall
caused by recent hard frost
paves the streets with gold

a young father
walks with son in backpack
my memories

slept in a bit
as body slowed by age
catches up

                    morning sunlight
                    grazes the autumn hills —
                    long shadows

        graceful bonsai
        elegant in autumn hues
        Japanese maple

day darkened with clouds
then night pulls back the gloom —
grinning crescent moon

ancient bugles
above a distant marsh
cranes

the locust trees
scatter their small gold coins
on walks and street

                    tonight's harvest moon
                    silvers alabaster clouds
                    celestial magic

her grace, that walk
awakened life in me —
then she was gone

of my God I know
she loves fields of wildflowers
and long star-filled nights

                                    a large gray cat strolls
                                    the street in front of my car
                                    tail high with disdain

murder of crows
plays on the winter wind
joy surfing

                    into the dark
                    gold wolf moon rises
                    Sirius howls

        luminous sky
        long thin clouds of coral
        quiet sunset

we walk in snow
the pup lifts his leg . . .marks
with yellow snow

                                        I wake at five
                                        the light on the ceiling
                                        has changed to snow

fading blue
tic-tac-toed in pink
sundown contrails

                    autumn sunrise
                  brushes a faint pink wash
                  on snowy peaks

        clearing the trees
        Orion's three-starred belt
        winter's scout

white chiffon
morphs to soft pink wool
winter sunset

                        light snow
                        starts in the morning
                        fills the day

sun warms the day
melts the new fallen snow
and downspout sings

        a winter wind
        filled with dry bits of fall
        bites to the bone

childhood memory
muted sound of the snow plow
passing in the dark

petals folded
alley sunflowers'
graceful death mask

golden sparks
flying from crow's wings
at sunset

at the close
of the warm winter day
a soft rain

                          starts at minus five
                          the day warms to plus eight
                          only the crows fly

on winter walk
a summer voice laughing
chatty nuthatch

bright quarter moon
drags the ash tree shadows
across the snow

                          a morning contrail
                          morphs into feathered cirrus
                          nature's fine brushwork

the new snow
squeaks under my boots
as if alive

                    good snowmelt —
                    three of pup's plush toys
                    found alive

winged bits of night
glide through tree tops to roosts
winter day's close

crows and gulls
fly through snow and fog
black and white scene

a lonely goose
calls from the winter sky
where is its mate

two bare elms
suddenly black with leaves
murder of crows

                eighteen-month-old girl
                takes and holds my finger
                leaves with my heart

beyond gray clouds
orange flames turn soft pink
desert sunrise

through low fog
the sun's a silver disk
winter magic

                              the sky closed in
                              brought softly falling snow
                              filling the day

today I write
haiku with fourth grade kids
a day of fun

        low out-of-round moon
        its surface cracked by branches
        floods young night with light

the lone crow
flaps across a gray sky
calls once

moonlight reflects
off new fallen snow
a Buson scene

                                    some poets meet
                                    to read and share their work
                                    evening of fun

Orion trails
Luna who strolls with Mars
through winter night

               tonight Luna's
               in the arms of Orion
               fickle woman

parking lot lamp posts
with white and black finials
a gull and a crow

in fading light
silent crows fly to roost
gather their clans

                                west wind wafts
                                scent of western stock show
                                eau de cowlogne

in the kitchen
an explosion of color
amaryllis

                    night's warm rain
                    lies frozen at the curbs
                    winter stunned

Jupiter photos
show graceful swirls in color
van Gogh-like splendor

amazing building
aligned to summer solstice
spirits still live there

in Starbucks
mom and daughter boogie
to jingle bells

for a few seconds
the ponderosas burn gold
lit by sunset's match

                the moon danced
                across new year's eve sky
                with Orion

      winter sunset
      glows through leaf-bare tree tops
      evening lace

end of fall —
the solstice flings snow
winter and wind

clouds lower sky
shorten prairie view
shrink the world

blazing sunrise
softens to orange
day's quiet start

phantom bird
flies through heavy snow
spirit magpie

city noises
muffled by morning snow
childhood memories

the winter wind
packs the snow in drifts
with graceful curves

mountain wind
two dozen frolicking crows
surf the gusts

About the Author

Art Elser is a poet and writer who has been published in many journals and anthologies. His books include a memoir, *What's It All About, Alfie?*, and five books of poetry, *We Leave the Safety of the Sea, A Death at Tollgate Creek, As The Crow Flies, To See a World in a Grain of Sand,* and *It Seemed Innocent Enough.* Art lives in Denver with his wife, Kathy, and their pup, Walker.

www.ingramcontent.com/pod-product-compliance
Lightning Source LLC
Chambersburg PA
CBHW020429010526
44118CB00010B/488